PENGUINS: Unusual Birds

by Robert Cutting

TABLE OF CONTENTS

HOW PENGUINS MOVE

Penguins are birds. They have feathers and wings and lay eggs. Unlike most birds, though, penguins cannot fly, at least not in the air. Their wings actually look more like flippers. Some people say that penguins *do* fly, but in the water.

Scientists report that penguins could fly at one time—over 40 million years ago. As they spent more and more time in the ocean, their bodies adapted to life in water.

Penguins are known as **aquatic** birds. They swim, dive, float, row, play, and feed in the ocean. They are very suited to living in the water, since their bodies are shaped like little rockets. It is this shape that helps them twist and turn and fly through the waves.

Penguins look awkward on land, and can't move as easily as they do in the water. Penguins stand upright because their legs are set far back in their bodies. They waddle rather than walk because their legs are so short and stubby.

Some penguins, such as the Adelies, *will* walk hundreds of kilometres to their **rookery**. This is the place where they will lay their eggs and where the babies will hatch.

WINGS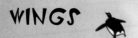

Penguins have wings that over the years have become more like flippers. They use their flippers to swim in the water, and will row with them when they are on the water's surface.

Penguins use their flippers to help them "toboggan" on their bellies across the snow. They will also wave their flippers and call out to find their mates. Penguins will sometimes shake their flippers, as though scolding, at other penguins who might try to steal their nesting stones. They will slap at sea gulls who swoop down to steal their chicks.

FEATHERS

Penguins have many layers of feathers that overlap to keep water away from their skin, much like scales do on fish. They also have **down** on the shafts of their feathers and this helps to keep them warm, since the penguins spend so much time in the water. The penguin's feathers need special care, and penguins are experts at **preening**.

When a penguin preens, it takes oil from a gland near its tail and spreads this all over its feathers. This makes its feathery coat waterproof and shiny.

Penguins **molt** once a year. Their old feathers wear out and drop off. The new feathers grow in within thirty days. While they are waiting for their new coat of feathers, penguins must stay out of the water. This means they cannot feed. To prepare for this, penguins build up a huge layer of fat under their skin.

SIZE

Penguins come in all sizes. Some are among the largest birds in the world. The emperor and king penguins are the biggest. Emperors are often as tall as 1.2 m and weigh about 40 kg. King penguins can weigh up to 18 kg and grow to 80 to 90 cm tall.

Fairy penguins are the smallest members of the penguin group. They have been called "little blues" because their feathers are bluish in colour. Fairy penguins grow to about 40 cm and weigh about 1 kg. They swim to shore each night to sleep. On the beaches of Australia, where these penguins live, people often gather to watch these little birds parade off to their nests.

EMPEROR PENGUINS
1.2 m

FAIRY
PENGUIN
40 cm

WHERE PENGUINS LIVE

Most people think of penguins living only in the cold places on Earth. It's true that many penguins, like the emperors and Adelies, live in the harsh conditions of Antarctica. Here the wind howls, snow swirls, and temperatures often reach a bone-chilling −62°C!

Other species like the warmer weather in places like the Galápagos Islands in the Pacific Ocean. Here the land is warm, although the water is chilled by cold currents. Black-footed penguins live on the coastal regions of South Africa. The temperature there can get very hot, and for this reason they build their nests underground to protect their young from the heat.

FOOD

No matter where they live in the world, all penguins feed in the oceans. They dive in to catch squid, fish, and **krill**. They use this food for themselves, as well as their young.

They feed their young with partly-digested material from their catch. During courtship, many penguins stop feeding until the courtship has ended and eggs have been laid.

14

ENEMIES

Penguins are very protective of their young and constantly watch for **predators** such as sea gulls and leopard seals. They will circle their nests and chase the predators away. In the water, penguins must be on the lookout for killer whales who wait for any unsuspecting bird to swim by.

15

KINDS OF PENGUINS

Penguins come in many **species**. Different penguin species can be detected by certain markings.

The Adelie, the chinstrap, and the gentoo species of penguins all have stiff, brushlike tails.

Adelies

These penguins have black heads, and white rings appear around their eyes during the breeding season. They live in the ocean in Antarctica, staying in the water until breeding time, when they climb onto the land. They slide across the ice to find their rookeries. Penguin mates work together to prepare the nest. After the eggs are laid, both parents will spend time looking after their young.

Chinstraps

Chinstraps get their name from the thin black line that runs across their chins. Adelie and chinstrap penguins often use the same rookery areas. The chinstraps sometimes force the Adelies out of their nests so they can live there themselves. After breeding season, the chinstraps return to the ocean.

Gentoos

Gentoos have distinctive markings—red beaks, and white patches over the eyes. They are gentle creatures, unlike the chinstraps. They are large birds, frequently as heavy as 7 kg, and they stand almost 1 m high. Gentoos are the fastest swimmers among the many penguin species.

Rockhoppers

Rockhoppers are a kind of crested penguin that have tufts of orange or yellow hair sticking out over their red eyes. They are known as "rockhoppers" because they bounce like balls as they jump from rock to rock. When they dive into the ocean, they hop feet first.

Emperors

Emperors, the largest of all the penguin species, are quite majestic. They live in Antarctica and, unlike other penguins, they don't make nests. When an egg is laid, the male bird keeps it on his feet and protects it with a flap from his stomach. The female goes out into the ocean searching for food, and stays in the water until the egg hatches. When she returns, both parents take turns feeding and caring for the young chick.

DANGERS

At one time penguins were hunted for their oil, but today they are protected by law. Water that has been polluted by chemicals and oil spills poses new dangers for them. Overfishing in their traditional home waters has also resulted in many penguin species becoming **endangered**.

Today, many people are working hard to help these unusual birds live safely in their natural habitat.

GLOSSARY

aquatic   lives in the water

down   soft, fluffy feathers

endangered   a species of animal in danger
                  of disappearing from Earth

krill   small, shrimp-like ocean creatures

molt   to shed old feathers and grow
                  new ones

predators   animals or birds that feed on other
                  animals and birds

preening   cleaning of feathers with the
                  beak or bill

rookery   nesting place where penguins
                  lay eggs and raise their young

species   a type or grouping of an animal

24